BREATHIN

CW00435541

BREATHING DEEP

LIFE IN THE SPIRIT OF EASTER

Ian Adams

CANTERBURY
PRESS

Norwich

© Ian Adams 2018

First published in 2018 by the Canterbury Press Norwich
Editorial office
3rd Floor, Invicta House
108–114 Golden Lane
London EC1Y 0TG, UK

www.canterburypress.co.uk

Canterbury Press is an imprint of Hymns Ancient & Modern Ltd
(a registered charity)

Hymns Ancient & Modern® is a registered trademark of
Hymns Ancient & Modern Ltd
13A Hellesdon Park Road, Norwich,
Norfolk NR6 5DR, UK

All rights reserved. No part of this publication may be reproduced,
stored in a retrieval system, or transmitted, in any form or by any means,
electronic, mechanical, photocopying or otherwise, without the prior
permission of the publisher, Canterbury Press.

The Author has asserted his right under the Copyright, Designs and
Patents Act 1988 to be identified as the Author of this Work

Scripture quotations are from the New Revised Standard Version of the
Bible, Anglicized Edition, copyright © 1989, 1995 by the Division of
Christian Education of the National Council of the Churches of Christ
in the USA. Used by permission. All rights reserved.

British Library Cataloguing in Publication data

A catalogue record for this book is available from the British Library

978 1 78622 011 0

breath is life

CONTENTS

INTRODUCTION x

POEM: BEACH MASS xiv

THE RESURRECTION OF JESUS 2

[01] LET GO OF YOUR SADNESS 4

[02] WHO ARE YOU LOOKING FOR? 6

[03] HEAR YOUR NAME SPOKEN IN LOVE 8

[04] LET ME GO 10

[05] DO NOT BE AFRAID 12

[06] LOOK FOR THE CHRIST 14

[07] ONE GOES AHEAD OF YOU 16

[08] WALK TOGETHER 18

[09] HEAR THE QUESTIONS BEING ASKED 20

[10] WHAT ARE YOU TALKING ABOUT? 22

[11] STAY WITH US 24

[12] BLESS BREAD, SHARE IT 26

[13] OPEN YOUR EYES TO WHAT IS 28

[14] RECOGNIZE THE CHRIST 30

[15] PEACE BE WITH YOU (I) 32

[16] WHAT ARE YOU AFRAID OF? 34

we dream of a better world

[17] SKIN TO SKIN   36

[18] TELL THE STORY   38

[19] WAIT FOR STRENGTH   40

[20] RECEIVE BLESSING   42

[21] LIVE FROM YOUR JOY   44

[22] RETREAT   46

[23] PEACE BE WITH YOU (II)   48

[24] RECEIVE THE HOLY SPIRIT   50

[25] IF YOU FORGIVE   52

[26] IF YOU RETAIN   54

[27] PEACE BE WITH YOU (III)   56

[28] REACH OUT   58

[29] GO DEEPER   60

[30] SIT WITH ME   62

[31] LOVE ME (I)   64

[32] LOVE ME (II)   66

[33] LOVE ME (III)   68

[34] CARE FOR THESE   70

[35] FOLLOW ME   72

[36] WAIT FOR THE DIVINE REVEALING   74

[37] BECOME A GIFT TO THOSE AROUND YOU   76

[38] SEE RESURRECTION IN EVERYTHING   78

[39] IMMERSE YOURSELF   80

[40] GO!   82

IDEAS FOR REFLECTION AND ACTION   84

© text and photography by Ian Adams

we will need to breathe deep

INTRODUCTION

We dream of a better world. More peaceful, hopeful and generous. And despite appearances, such a world is possible. Here and now. In these demanding times. But such a world must take shape first within us. And it will require much of us. We will need to breathe deep.

Breath is life. The first breath taken by the newborn child is a moment of wonder. Our last breath a gateway into something unknown. Across the spiritual traditions practices of stillness and contemplation invariably give attention to the breath. In breathing practice we recognize the patterns that shape us. Here we are vulnerable. But here too is strength. We learn to be present. We draw on the great Life that is the source of all being.

Breathing Deep draws on themes and phrases from the stories told in the gospels about the resurrection of Jesus. About his return to breath, about his breathing deep. From the time of their writing and first telling, those stories have been seen as invitations to allow the resurrection to reshape the way that life can be lived. This work looks again at those invitations, and imagines them as gifts for us now, opening up the possibility of something new.

If you happen to be reading this in the Easter season after the toughness of Lent, the space these invitations offer may be welcome. But they also come with a provocative edge. Can we find the courage to live in the spirit of resurrection when everything seems to gravitate towards death and destruction?

The resurrection of Jesus was an extraordinary happening in history. But deep in the Christ tradition it has always been understood as more than a one-off event, and seen rather as a glimpse into the true nature of everything. This is not just resurrection as past event or future consummation (though both are vital elements) but resurrection as revealing the true nature of existence, in which birth, life, death and resurrection are all always connected and always moving forward.

to live in the spirit of resurrection

The core of each of these reflections was written in real time in the Easter season. For 40 days I attempted to let the resurrection story work on me. And the heart of each reflection remains here as it was written then, retaining the raw surprise – the breathing deep – of the Easter experience as I let it work on me. Our human stories, of course, have much in common, and I hope that you will find something of yourself here. I hope too that you will find something to encourage you on the path we are taking together towards a better world for all, here and now.

The meditations can be followed through from 1 to 40, but they can also be used on their own, or mixed and matched. The series works well for both individual reflection and in a group setting with space for conversation, response and creative action.

Each reflection is accompanied by a line from Psalm 116, 117 or 118. Jesus would have almost certainly have known the Psalms by heart, and we can imagine him praying these psalms of joy and thanksgiving.

The images for the series are all from islands of the Inner Hebrides off the west coast of mainland Scotland. As a result of centuries of poverty and depopulation there is a sense of sadness present in these lands and seascapes. There's also great beauty here, and for me a sense of connection to those who have tried to live here in the spirit of resurrection long before us. To breathe deep here, to sense renewed at-oneness with machair and ocean, with sea-eagle and with saint is a sustaining gift. I hope that the vibrancy of these images convey something of that Easter spirit.

With Mary Magdalene and 'the other Mary' – those earliest witnesses to the resurrection of Jesus – may we sense together a new joy for what may be coming into being.

Breathe deep.

you may find something of yourself here

BEACH MASS

In kind evening light. A softening for the day's sharp edges. We skimmed smooth stones for our becoming. Each touch, each splash, each skip a track to follow. Gathering storm-bleached sticks in a circle of pebbles we laid a fire. As supper cooked bread was passed round. Wine was poured. And under a night sky bright with dreams from forever we found ourselves again. To the wind song's chimes we told our stories and made our prayers and gave our thanks. Then settled in the lengthening pause between words. Between breaths. Between life as is. And life as may yet be. All became still. All became one. A beach mass for the spinning world.

settle in the pause

THE RESURRECTION OF JESUS

Matthew 28.1–10 (NRSV)

After the sabbath, as the first day of the week was dawning, Mary Magdalene and the other Mary went to see the tomb. And suddenly there was a great earthquake; for an angel of the Lord, descending from heaven, came and rolled back the stone and sat on it. His appearance was like lightning, and his clothing white as snow. For fear of him the guards shook and became like dead men. But the angel said to the women, 'Do not be afraid; I know that you are looking for Jesus who was crucified. He is not here; for he has been raised, as he said. Come, see the place where he lay. Then go quickly and tell his disciples, "He has been raised from the dead, and indeed he is going ahead of you to Galilee; there you will see him." This is my message for you.' So they left the tomb quickly with fear and great joy, and ran to tell his disciples. Suddenly Jesus met them and said, 'Greetings!' And they came to him, took hold of his feet, and worshiped him. Then Jesus said to them, 'Do not be afraid; go and tell my brothers to go to Galilee; there they will see me.'

do not be afraid

[01] LET GO OF YOUR SADNESS

Can you see how you hold on to your sadness?
How you keep it tucked away in case of need.
You nurture it, giving the pot an occasional stir.
Fermenting some dark brew.

Sadness is part of the human condition.
And it is the necessary companion to happiness.
Together, in time, they will bring into being some glorious
    new thing,
as yet unimagined.

You were not made for sadness alone.
Can you allow your anguish and your yearning
to open up your joy?

On this day of resurrection,
on this day of possibility,
on this new day,
let go of your sadness.

Just for a day.
And see what flows from it.
Then tomorrow, if you can, do the same.
And then the next day.

One day at a time.
Let go of your sadness.

this is the Lord's doing;
it is marvellous in our eyes
Psalm 118.23

[02] WHO ARE YOU LOOKING FOR?

Don't answer too fast.

You scan your horizons.
Are you searching to find yourself,
seeking your place of belonging?
Yes, of course.

Recognize that you are also, increasingly, seeking the Christ.

And although he remains for the most part
seemingly hidden, reticent and undisclosed
you also sense that the Christ is seeking you,
close and curious.

So the seeker is sought.

And whoever you are looking for
is already here.

Close to you, curious.

he has heard my voice
Psalm 116.1

[03] HEAR YOUR NAME SPOKEN IN LOVE

This is what you have always wanted.

Part of your story is the sifting of the many sounds
for the one sound.
The sound of your name, spoken in love.
And here it is.
Early morning, in a garden.

But you have never felt entirely at home with your name.
You would have called *you* something else.
So what to make of this, the calling of your name?

There is no reticence in the speaker's voice.
It is your name, for better, or for worse, and for now.
And it is a name that points to the reality of who you are,
but does not diminish you.

There is another name that is yours beyond time,
a name that will be revealed to you,
etched, the story goes, onto a stone.
That will be yours, always.

But for here and for now,
hear your name spoken, in love.

I will call on him as long as I live
Psalm 116.2

[04] LET ME GO

Don't hold on to me.
Let me go.

It's a strange invitation.
Feels more like a reprimand.
And so it may be.
Is it possible that you have been holding too closely
to your idea of the Christ?

This invitation may be to let the Christ be the Christ.
Far more than your imagination has allowed to this point.

Freedom is at the heart of love.
And you may only truly love when you learn to let go.
To allow the other to be fully themselves.

So allow the Christ to be the Christ.
As the Christ allows you to be you.

Let me go.

the snares of death encompassed me
Psalm 116.3

[05] DO NOT BE AFRAID

Have you noticed how fear is never far away?
And so destructive?

In the world around you.
But also within you.
How fear of what might happen seeps
into so much of your decision (and indecision) making.

This invitation is to let go of your fear.
To believe the best.
To be bold.
To face your fears with the love that flows
from resurrection.

You are beloved.
So love.
And do not be afraid.

gracious is the Lord, and righteous
Psalm 116.5

[06] LOOK FOR THE CHRIST

This is an invitation to seek the Christ.

To look for signs of his presence.
To move from vague awareness
to the more intentional possibility
of presence.

The seeking is not for proof, or for your own satisfaction.
But rather that in the seeking you will open yourself up
to a presence that is always present,
if often ignored.

And the tradition is clear –
this presence has both a personal
and a cosmic-all nature.

The risen Christ will be with us – *with you* – always.

He is close.
Look for the Christ.

our God is merciful
Psalm 116.5

[07] ONE GOES AHEAD OF YOU

You do not have to do this on your own.
The path has been trodden before.
One goes ahead of you.

All your doubts and fears,
spoken and unspoken,
have been experienced before.

Whatever you face has been faced.
Your questions about life and death.
And the personal stuff you are carrying with you.
That sack of stories.
All of it is shared.

This does not mean that everything is planned out for you.
But rather that the path will reveal itself
as you walk it.
With just the hint of another.
The outline of a footprint in the earth,
some clearing in the grass,
a fragrance.

So take the next step, with faith and hope and love.

One goes ahead of you.

the Lord protects the simple
Psalm 116.6

[08] WALK TOGETHER

You know the gifts of solitude.
You are happy with your own company.
You enjoy this quiet walking.

And it's good that you are working out how
to be aware and creative on your own.

But this invitation is to allow the company of another
to be a gift to you.
And to let them surprise you.

The particular surprise of the Gospel story
is that the other who walks with you
is as yet a stranger.

Can you let today's stranger walk with you?

Walk together.

when I was brought low, he saved me
Psalm 116.6

[09] HEAR THE QUESTIONS BEING ASKED

You have become adept at hearing your own questions.

The challenge now is to hear the questions that others
    are asking
– even if you do not understand or like their premise.

So what questions are being asked by those who – it seems to
    you – may be acting from their fear?
Or by those choosing to seek or confer the dangerous promise
    of power?
And how might you help them to recognize their fears
for what they are?

Imagine what you could do to enable a more compassionate
and hopeful response.

Hear the questions being asked.

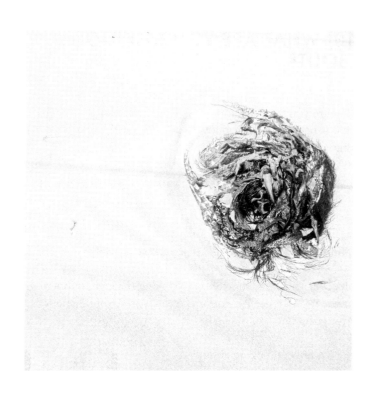

return, O my soul, to your rest
Psalm 116.7

[10] WHAT ARE YOU TALKING ABOUT?

What are you thinking about?
What is occupying your body, mind and spirit?
What are you talking about?

This invitation is to give voice to whatever is welling up
    within you.

To offer what resounds as a gift
– and to understand that it is part of your learning.

Whatever you are talking about, thinking through, pondering,
has the means to shape you – and the world around you –
    for good.

So what are you talking about?
And can you find the languages you need
to open up the conversation
both for you and for the people around you?

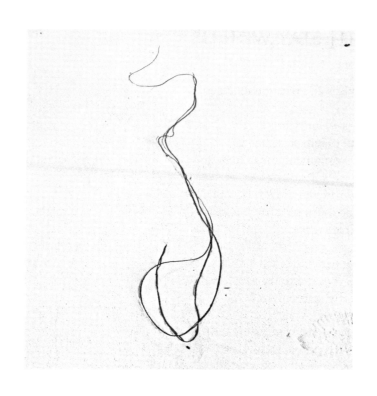

the Lord has dealt bountifully with you
Psalm 116.7

[11] STAY WITH US

This is an invitation to linger.

Not to hurry on.
But to remain.
For a moment, for an hour, for a day, for a season, for a lifetime.

You are doing a lot, hoping a lot, imagining a lot.
And much of what you are working on has a future impetus.
Which is fine.

But here's the invitation.
To you, and to the Christ within you.
Today, stay with us.

Give yourself to the moment.
To the people you are with.
To this small track of earth as you walk here.

Be present.
Stay with us.

you have delivered my soul from death
Psalm 116.8

[12] BLESS BREAD, SHARE IT

How easily we take food and drink for granted.

The invitation here is to become present to the food and
    the drink,
to the moment, and to the provider.

To give thanks for the food,
to bless it and to receive its blessing,
and to bless each other in the sharing.

Find beautiful words that open up the mystery.
Make them true to you.
Accessible to those sharing.
And reflective of the setting in which they are offered.

Bless bread.
Share it.

I will lift up the cup of salvation
Psalm 116.13

[13] OPEN YOUR EYES TO WHAT IS

You see what you want to see.
There's something good about that.
In that kind of seeing you are already re-shaping the world
as you long for it to be.

But the invitation (and challenge) is to see what truly is.

Look closely, deeply, carefully –
and both the wonder and toughness of everything
will be revealed.

This is a demanding task.
And your seeing will never be the same again.

you have delivered my eyes from tears
Psalm 116.8

[14] RECOGNIZE THE CHRIST

People can be a real disappointment.
You can be a real disappointment.

It can be hard to see the light in us or around us.
But the light is there.
And this invitation is to see the light.
To recognize the Christ.

In the other person.
Yes.
But also in yourself.
The Christ is present in you!

This may be the essential starting point.
You can only truly recognize the Christ in the other
when you begin to recognize – and give space to – the Christ
    in you.

O Lord I am your servant
Psalm 116.16

[15] PEACE BE WITH YOU (I)

You are a person of peace.
A peaceful peace-making person.
But you know the moments of unease and turmoil
that assail you.

The key to peace being truly experienced and shared
is for you to learn how to live from your peaceful centre.

Do not be afraid
comes the risen Christ's repeated message.
Peace be with you.

And this peace is a gift that is already yours.
You just need to locate it.
And allow it to flow in, around and through you.

Peace be with you.

great is his steadfast love towards us
Psalm 117.2

[16] WHAT ARE YOU AFRAID OF?

You are an optimistic person.
Hopeful, peaceful, happy.
And yet you have fears.

The question is revealing.
It implies that you need not be fearful.

But on what is this based?
That nothing should be feared?
No. There are many tough processes that deserve your fear.

That nothing can hurt you?
Unlikely – many things may hurt you.

That God will protect you from all that hurts?
Even in God's care life will bring loss.

The invitation to see your fears for what they are
is rooted in a whole different way of being.

Even in the midst of trial,
seeds of possibility are coming to life.
What are you afraid of?

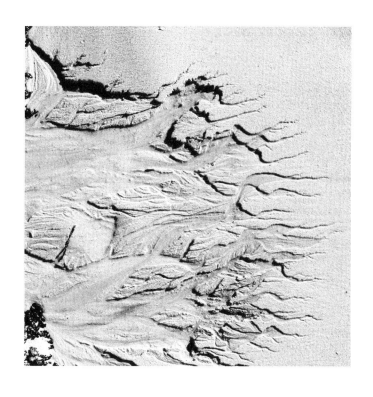

I will call on the name of the Lord
Psalm 116.17

[17] SKIN TO SKIN

This is an invitation that comes with risk.
To come skin to skin is to become vulnerable
to the touch of another.

Skin is earthy.
Skin is mess.
And skin is wonder.
A risk.

But for all these reasons
skin to skin is a joyous thing.
A coming home.

In the gift and grace of another, may you find yourself,
    skin to skin.

you have loosed my bonds
Psalm 116.16

[18] TELL THE STORY

Have you noticed how you sometimes keep the hope small?

How you can hold it to yourself, unwilling or unable
to allow its gift to emerge.
Gazing at the light of the small screen in your hand.
When on some hill top a beacon awaits your lighting.

This is an invitation to step into the story.
It has to be lived if it is to be told with authenticity.
It must be yours.
So that you can speak it without notes.
From the heart.
All flame.

You are always looking for the language that will connect.
Good.
Keep on doing that.
But even more important is the gift of a story that is lived
    and loved.
Then the language you use will come
– and will be received – very naturally.

Tell the story.
Light a beacon fire.

praise the Lord, all you nations!
Psalm 117.1

[19] WAIT FOR STRENGTH

Don't force the future.

Wait for the strength that you will need
to do whatever must be done.
At the right time, it will be yours.

As if from on high

strength

will

descend

and

settle upon you.

Wait for strength. Then rise.

the faithfulness of the Lord endures forever
Psalm 117.2

[20] RECEIVE BLESSING

You are focused on your intention.

To help to reshape the world for good.
To enable blessing and to bring blessing.
Good.
But this is an invitation to *receive* blessing.

So let the blessing come to you.
Allow yourself to be nurtured.

The God of blessing wishes this.
For you.
And for the world.

Receive blessing.
Let the light of blessing
fall on you.

O give thanks to the Lord for he is good
Psalm 118.1

[21] LIVE FROM YOUR JOY

Are you ready for a demanding gift?

Something that will – if you allow it – transform everything.

The gift is joy, and it is already yours.
Not something that needs grasping for,
not something dependent on things going well
(always a transitory state of being.)

Patient and generous, joy waits within you.
The joy is already yours.

What is the demand of this gift?
The demand is the realization that you have some choice.

Joy is not forced upon you.
Occasionally it will be poured upon you.
Most of the time it is humble and shy.
But it is there.
And waiting for you to choose.

Will you live today from your joy?

his steadfast love endures forever
Psalm 118.1

[22] RETREAT

Close the door.

Step into the cell of your monastic.
Enter the garden of your mystic.

Away from all the busyness.
For a while, leave all that behind.
Retreat.

This may at first be humiliating, even painful
as you are confronted by all your chaos and noise.
But persist.
Recognize the patterns, then let them fall away.

Winter night. Be held in the warm cell.
Spring morning. Let the light find you.
Summer day. Walk in the cool garden.
Autumn evening. Love calls love.

Let each season gift you the love that cannot be contained.
The love that persists.

Retreat.

out of my distress I called on the Lord
Psalm 118.5

[23] PEACE BE WITH YOU (II)

What an invitation!
This is the path to change.
For you and for the world.

St Seraphim urges you
Acquire inner peace,
and around you thousands will find their salvation …

It's as simple – and as demanding as that.
The experience of peace being with you is a choice.
It is there waiting for you.
Whenever you remember to access it –
and increasingly as it becomes your unconscious way of being.

Every day, every decision, every difficulty
is a new opportunity to be in peace.

Choose peace.
Peace will choose you.
And the world will be changed for good.

the Lord answered me,
and set me in a broad place
Psalm 118.5

[24] RECEIVE THE HOLY SPIRIT

Every day the invitation comes.

Receive the Holy Spirit.

Let the divine Spirit flow in and around you
flooding you with grace and with love,
with wisdom and with imagination,
with hope and with strength.

And all that is required of you is assent.
Openness.
Let the Spirit come.

Allow yourself to be drawn deeper into the life of the Trinity.
And into the life of the world.

I was falling, but the Lord helped me
Psalm 118.13

[25] IF YOU FORGIVE

If you forgive
the people you forgive
will be forgiven.

And the world will be changed a little for good.
The ripples will spread.
And the water of reconciliation will lap generously
on the shores of your world.

So who do you need to forgive?
Name them.
With compassion.

And yourself?

For all my missteps and mistakes.

I forgive.
I forgive.
I forgive.

it is better to take refuge in the Lord
Psalm 118.8

[26] IF YOU RETAIN

What are you holding onto that could be let go?
Is a good question.
But what sins – if any – need holding on to?
And how could that be an invitation?

There may be sins that need retaining, remembering, holding
    on to.
The sins that deal death and destruction.
These sins should not be ignored, forgotten or forgiven
(even as we seek the grace to forgive their perpetrators).

Allow the energy in their retention
to envision and empower you to work for change.

I shall recount the deeds of the Lord
Psalm 118.17

[27] PEACE BE WITH YOU (III)

This moment.

Is where peace begins.

Imagine.
A pebble
dropping
into
still water.

A splash, then ripples, and a deep calm.
The surface skitters in the breeze.
A feather drops and is held by the water's shining skin.

The deep water is still.
Supporting everything that moves on the surface.
Reflecting the beauty of movement above it.

Find your deep pool.
Your tranquility.
Your peace.

the Lord is my strength
Psalm 118.14

[28] REACH OUT

Life has an internal dimension.
Only you can know what it is to be you.
To know what it is to exist you have to go inwards.
The inner path requires your commitment.

But an invitation comes to reach out.
To experience the sacrament of life
in engagement with whatever and whoever is around you.
To make the outer journey.

To touch the beautiful and broken body of the world
and there to discover the Christ
in all and for all.

So reach out.

there are glad songs
Psalm 118.15

[29] GO DEEPER

You love so many things.
The world around is full of delight.
Photography, music, poetry, film, food and drink,
landscape and cityscape.

The invitation now is to go deeper.
And in order to truly experience the mystery
you may need to find it in *a few* things.
Or even for a season
in the *one* thing.

Give yourself to these few,
or to this one thing.
And go deeper.

In this sharper focus let the true depths of existence be
    revealed.
The tragedy and the wonder of it all.
Go deeper.

open to me the gates of righteousness
Psalm 118.19

[30] SIT WITH ME

There's something so welcoming in this invitation.
So simple and so nourishing.
Sit here with me. Eat with me. Join me.

The invitation is to sit with the Christ.

To receive from him.
To share whatever is nurturing him.
To enter deeper into companionship.
Into at-oneness.

At the start of the day.
During the day.
At the end of the day.
Sit with me.

that I may give thanks to the Lord
Psalm 118.19

[31] LOVE ME (I)

In the gospel this is posed as a question.
Do you love me?
But for you, today, it is in invitation.
And one that may open up a new way of being.

Love for Jesus the Christ
is the beginning
of a pathway into a wider love.

Into love for the earth and her creatures.
Into love for neighbour and stranger.
Into love for the saints.
Into love for God.

It's an invitation that cannot be accepted tentatively.
It requires your whole being.
Your all.
And like almost all these invitations it begins now.
And continues moment by moment.

Love me.

this is the gate of the Lord
Psalm 118.20

[32] LOVE ME (II)

Love me.

Love me by loving
this street,
these people,
this moment.

And in loving this street, these people and this moment in time
you are loving me.

Give yourself to them, and so to me.
Sense my presence.
All around you.

The quiet centre towards which everything is moving.
Love me.

you have become my salvation
Psalm 118.21

[33] LOVE ME (III)

Love me.
By loving yourself.

I am in you, you in me.
Your divine nature – however hidden – is a beautiful reality.

How can you not love yourself?
You are a beautiful creation, a being of delight and love.

So love yourself.
And allow me to love you through that love.

As you learn to love yourself,
so your love will grow for the world around you.

Love yourself.
Love the world.
Love me.

I love the Lord
Psalm 116.1

[34] CARE FOR THESE

Some days you wake in disquiet; a weight heavy upon you.
Your semi-conscious full of foreboding.
An electric fence humming.

This is one those days.
A sick feeling at the nature of the society of which you
    are part.
Foreboding has become reality, leaving you numb.
Your first instinct is to plot your leaving.
To somewhere more caring,
more imaginative,
more free.

Yet it's into *this* setting that the invitation comes.
Care for the people around you, care for these.

Focus your love and your energy
on the people you encounter today
where you are.

Care for these.

this is the day that the Lord has made
Psalm 118.24

[35] FOLLOW ME

You don't have to forge your own path.
It's not all down to you.

Follow me.
I've taken this path – and the paths you may yet take –
    before you.

I am with you on the road.
I am beside you.
And I am ahead of you.
Follow me.

Not from a distance.
But close.
So close that you can sense my breathing, and I yours.

Follow me.

blessed is the one who comes in the name of the Lord
Psalm 118.26

[36] WAIT FOR THE DIVINE REVEALING

There is no rush.
Allow time to become a gift.
Accept slow.
And wait.

Wait for the right time.
Wait for the divine revealing.
Wait for the Holy Spirit.

And allow yourself to be drawn in close.
Your spirit and the Holy Spirit
in a dance of life, of love, and of light.

Wait for the Holy Spirit.

the Lord is God, and he has given us light
Psalm 118.27

[37] BECOME A GIFT TO THOSE AROUND YOU

Sometimes you slip into preoccupation with yourself.
With your life, your direction, your losses and your findings.

The invitation here is to look outwards.
To become a gift, a gift to those around you.

And you will become a gift by becoming truly the person
    you are.
By living the life that has always been waiting within you.

Your life aligned towards your true North
will be a life that offers hope for others.

Love for God and love for neighbour will become as one.
And quietly you will become a gift to all around you.

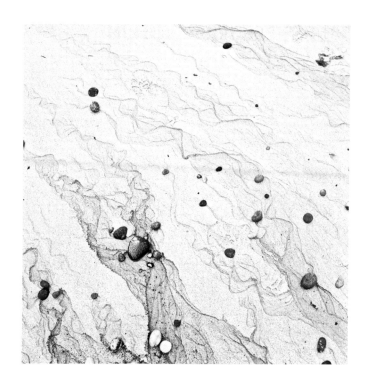

in the presence of all his people
Psalm 116.18

[38] SEE RESURRECTION IN EVERYTHING

Resurrection is not only a future hope.
It happens now.
Vibrant and inextinguishable.

And small signs of resurrection are everywhere.
In the street where you live.
In imaginative design.
In the patient turning of the seasons.
In courageous movements for justice,
And in the daily acts of devotion that so many will offer
to God and neighbour today.

The invitation is to see resurrection.
To allow the resurrection to seep into your life.
To embody resurrection.
So that you live resurrection life now.

the stone that the builders rejected
has become the chief cornerstone
Psalm 118.22

[39] IMMERSE YOURSELF

You believe (as much as you can) and you are baptized.
So what is the invitation here?

Baptism takes cerebral belief into the experienced reality
   of water.
Might it be time to be immersed again in faith and its outcomes?

To abandon yourself to the love of God in whom you live.
To entrust yourself to the depths of unknowing.
And to hear that you too are beloved.

See each choice today as another small baptism.
Another immersion into the life of God.

In the name of the Father.
and of the Son.
and of the Holy Spirit.

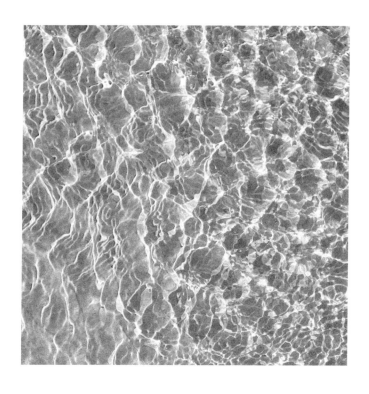

you are my God, and I will give thanks to you
Psalm 118.28

[40] GO!

You could stay here.

But the invitation is to go.
This may or may not involve a physical move.
But you are being asked to give yourself with devotion
to what lies ahead of you.

To live in the spirit of resurrection
wherever you are called.

With St Brendan to abandon the comforts of home.
To leave the shores of your experience.
And to set out on the ocean that is calling you.

In this endeavour you will not be alone.
The Christ's *Go!* is always a *Come!*

O give thanks to the Lord, for he is good;
for his steadfast love endures forever
Psalm 118.29

IDEAS FOR REFLECTION AND ACTION

LECTIO DIVINA

1 Read a passage from one of the gospel narratives of the resurrection of Jesus.
2 What catches your attention?
3 How might this (whatever has caught your attention) be a gift to you at this time?
4 Pray with the phrase that has caught your attention, allowing it to carry all your hopes and prayers.
5 Let the phrase fall away – enter stillness.

40 INVITATIONS

1 Read one of the 40 Invitations.
2 What (if anything) in this invitation resonates with your own experience?
3 What alternative or additional invitation do you sense may be present here?

CREATIVE RESPONSE

1 Take an episode from one of the accounts of the resurrection of Jesus – or a line from Psalm 116, 117 or 118 – and in response create a piece of art in your chosen field (painting, music, photography, poem, prose, drama, etc.)
2 You could set the piece in your own contemporary context.
3 Another option in a group setting is to invite everyone to choose a single phrase from one of the gospel narratives or from one of the suggested psalms to meditate on and then to create their work from that phrase.

opening up the possibility of something new